British Bombers
of World War I
in Action

By Peter Cooksley
Color by Don Greer

Squadron/Signal Publications

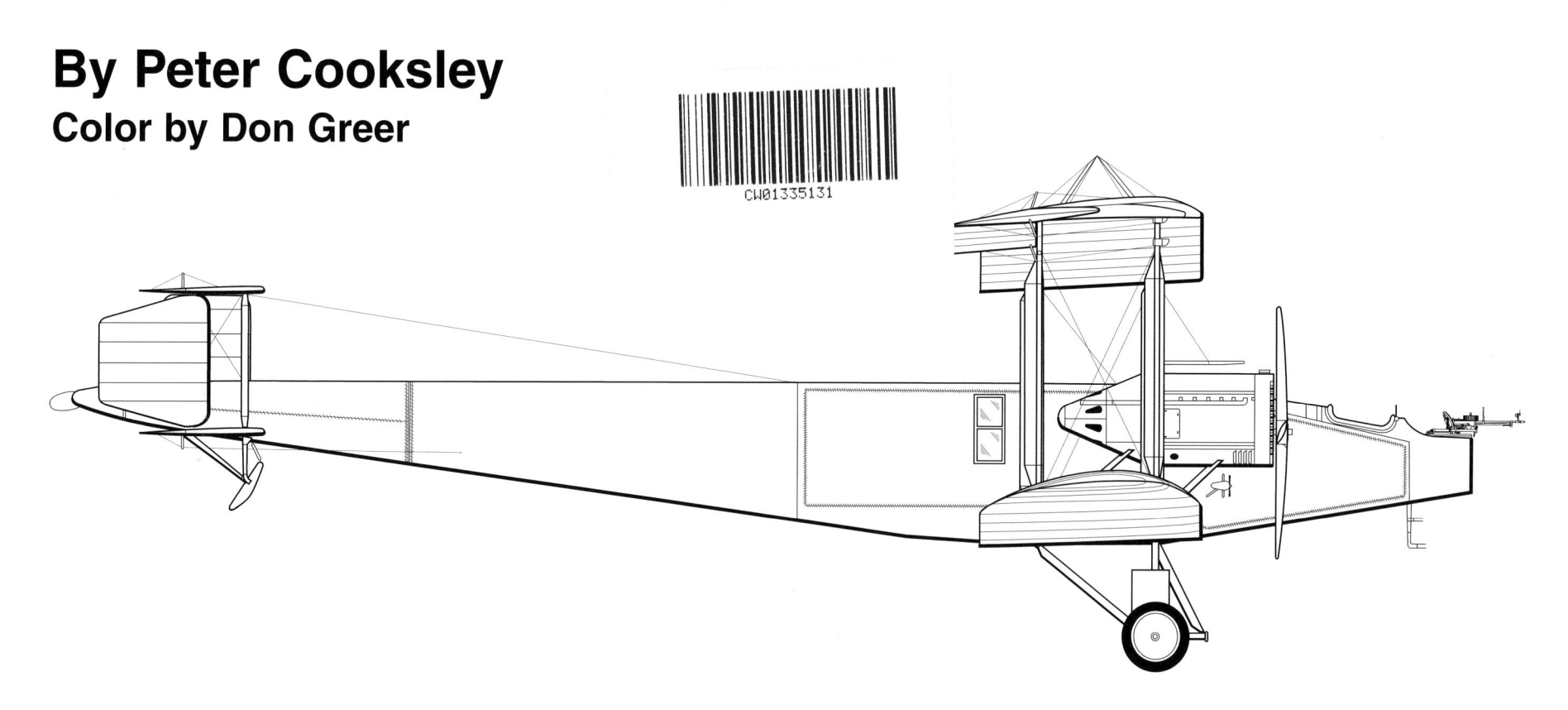

Aircraft Number 202

Cover: Vickers Vimy IV H652 on a postwar test flight. One of ten Vimys built at the Royal Aeronautical Establishment, Farnborough, H652 was originally F2916 and powered by Fiat engines before conversion to Roll-Royce Eagles.

Acknowledgements

The author gives grateful thanks for the opportunity to augment the photographs from his collection with contributions to these pages by Bruce Robertson, V. J. Garwood and Chaz Bowyer.

COPYRIGHT 2006 SQUADRON/SIGNAL PUBLICATIONS
1115 CROWLEY DRIVE CARROLLTON, TEXAS 75011-5010
All rights reserved. No part of this publication may be reproduced, stored in a retrieval system, or transmitted in any form by means electrical, mechanical, or otherwise, without written permission of the publisher.

ISBN 0-89747-505-4

If you have any photographs of aircraft, armor, soldiers or ships of any nation, particularly wartime snapshots, why not share them with us and help make Squadron/Signal's books all the more interesting and complete in the future? Any photograph sent to us will be copied and the original returned. The donor will be fully credited for any photos used. Please send them to:

Squadron/Signal Publications, Inc.
1115 Crowley Drive
Carrollton, TX 75011-5010

Если у вас есть фотографии самолётов, вооружения, солдат или кораблей любой страны, особенно, снимки времён войны, поделитесь с нами и помогите сделать новые книги издательства Эскадрон/Сигнал ещё интереснее. Мы перенимем ваши фотографии и вернём оригиналы. Имена приславших снимки будут сопровождать все опубликованные фотографии. Пожалуйста, присылайте фотографии по адресу:

Squadron/Signal Publications, Inc.
1115 Crowley Drive
Carrollton, TX 75011-5010

軍用機、装甲車両、兵士、軍艦などの写真を所持しておられる方はいらっしゃいませんか？どの国のものでも結構です。作戦中に撮影されたものが特に良いのです。Squadron/Signal社の出版する刊行物において、このような写真は内容を一層充実し、興味深くすることができます。当方にお送り頂いた写真は、複写の後お返しいたします。出版物中に写真を使用した場合は、必ず提供者のお名前を明記させて頂きます。お写真は下記にご送付ください。

Squadron/Signal Publications, Inc.
1115 Crowley Drive
Carrollton, TX 75011-5010

▸ **A Handley Page O/400, as identified by the short engine nacelles that were the main recognition feature of the four hundred or so delivered before the Armistice. The O/100, of which only forty were built, had longer nacelles.**

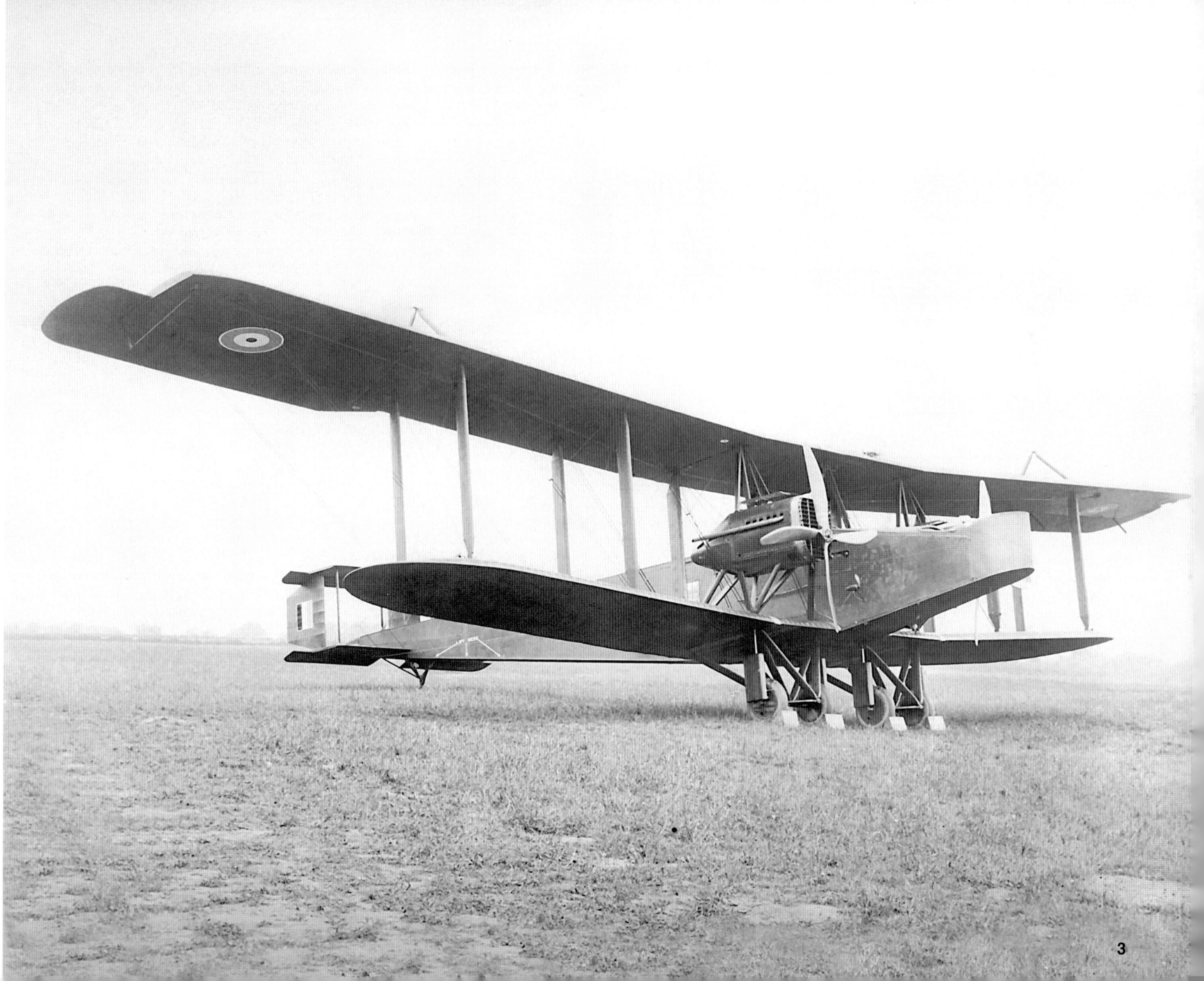

Introduction

As early as 1912, the Royal Navy had shown an interest in the potential of dropping bombs from aircraft. Some of the earliest experiments to determine the minimum safe altitude from which bombs could be dropped without damage to the attacking aircraft had been undertaken by that service. However, upon the outbreak of war in 1914, the only bomb to be had was the twenty-pound Hale bomb, and only twenty-six of these were immediately available. Despite this handicap, the Admiralty in London immediately began to look into the possibility of procuring a large airplane capable of making patrols to monitor the movements of U-boats and other vessels likely to interfere with the shipping lanes through which the greater part of Britain's food supply and raw materials were delivered.

The obvious source of such an airplane seemed to be Handley Page Ltd. Although it had been in existence for only five years, during which time it had built only small, single-engine aircraft, the company already had plans to construct a twin-engine biplane capable of crossing the Atlantic Ocean at perhaps eighty miles per hour. This was to be designated 'L/200,' following the Handley Page system of designations based on engine horsepower.

The L/200 was offered to the Admiralty as the basis of a maritime patrol aircraft. Instead, Captain Murray Sueter, director of the British Admiralty's Air Department, and his technical adviser, Harris Booth, demanded an airplane powered by two engines and having a wingspan of 114 feet, an aircraft capable not only of sea patrol but also bombing the German High Seas Fleet in Kiel harbor. Thus the Handley Page Type 'O' was created, and its basic design was largely agreed to by 4 February 1915.

This new design was powered by two 226-horsepower engines, and might have been called the 'O/200' (for its 200-plus horsepower engines) or even 'O/300' (the horsepower rounded up), as described unofficially on an old document. However, a designation based on engine power was seen as possibly conveying useful information to a potential enemy, and an official objection to it was lodged. Accordingly, the new aircraft was designated 'O/100,' adopting the now-reduced wingspan (one hundred feet) as part of the model designation.

The prototype of the new airplane, which first flew from Hendon on 18 December 1915, had a glazed nose extended back over the flight deck. A gun position was later substituted for the glazing, and most of the armor was removed.

The O/100 proved successful as both a bomber and maritime patrol aircraft, so it was logical that work should commence on a new and upgraded version to be known as the O/400, which began to appear in quantity during the spring of 1918. The O/400 strongly resembled the earlier O/100 except for the engines, but the new aircraft eliminated some of the earlier type's faults, such as the tail flutter experienced by a few O/100s. A redesigned aileron trailing edge also was introduced, effective with airframe number 1457.

The O/400 was used both for maritime patrols by the Royal Naval Air Service (RNAS) and regularly as a night bomber during the final three months of the war by the Royal Air Force's newly-constituted Independent Air Force (IAF). On a few occasions the IAF dropped 1,650-pound bombs on the Rhineland and Saar industrial areas; so great was the explosion from these "monster" weapons that the enemy at first mistook them for some type of linked cluster bomb.

A single example of the O/400 went to Palestine, where it was operated by No.1 Squadron, Australian Flying Corps. The United States also ordered 1,500 O/400s from the Standard Aircraft Corporation, J1934 being obtained from Harland and Wolf as a pattern for these.

Public indignation at air attacks on Britain were in part responsible for the Air Board ordering, as early as the second half of 1917, prototypes of a new generation of heavy bombers, again from Handley Page (the V/1500) and also from Vickers, Ltd. The latter's contribution, later known as the Vimy, caused astonishment when, during a test flight at Martlesham in January 1918, it proved capable of lifting a load greater than that of the much larger Handley Page O/400. Accordingly, an order for a hundred was immediately placed after three prototypes had been built. However, production was delayed by continual redesign of the aircraft for a variety of different engine installations, and as a result, the Vickers Vimy saw no action before the Armistice. Only one Vimy had reached the RAF's Independent Air Force at Nancy by the end of the war.

American interest in the Vimy extended to a specially-built version ordered with two 400-horsepower Liberty engines. The first of these was destroyed in a fire, with the result that subsequent work on the project was abandoned, and no Liberty-powered Vimy ever flew.

The Vimy was a contemporary of such bombers as the de Havilland D.H.10 and the Blackburn Kangaroo, both of which saw limited action. It epitomized the RAF's postwar bomber force and in small numbers also was to find a fresh lease of life as a civilian aircraft, as did the Handley Page O/400. However, the Vimy, although conceived as a bomber, is better remembered as the aircraft which was to fly across the Atlantic and to Australia in the immediate postwar years. (▶ 6)

The figure just visible under the nose of this Handley Page O/100 emphasizes the size of these aircraft in a view which also shows the opposite rotation of the type's propellers.

Development

Handley Page O/100 First Prototype

Handley Page O/100 Second Prototype

Handley Page O/100 Production Version

Handley Page O/400 Production Version

Handley Page V/1500

Handley Page O/7

Handley Page O/10

Vickers Vimy IV

Handley Page O/100

The development of Britain's new giant bomber was not without problems, not the least of which was that of starting the engines without the aid of mechanical assistance. Hand-starting at first was out of the question, as the propellers could not be reached from the ground. Eventually a double ramp was devised, over which ran a succession of ground crewmen who swung the propellers as they passed, thereby priming the engines so they could be started with the hand magneto. The elimination of the nose glazing gave the second prototype a downward-tapered nose. This vanished when a forward gun position was added. Surprisingly, few problems appear to have risen with the wing-folding gear despite its massive proportions.

Bad luck seemed to surround the O/100 when two, numbers 1462 and 1463, were sent to France on New Year's Day, 1917. Finding unbroken cloud over the English Channel, Sub-Lieutenant Sands, piloting 1462, eventually found Villacoublay with the aid of dead reckoning, but the crew of 1463 (Lieutenant Henry Connell Vereker, Lieutenant Hibbard, Leading Mechanics Kennedy and Wright, and First Class Air Mechanic W. W. Higby) became lost due to a faulty compass. In an attempt to discover their whereabouts, Vereker descended to an altitude of two hundred feet, but, finding no break in the cloud, climbed back to 6,000 feet and spent some time there before losing altitude again. As fuel began to run out, they spotted a church spire and landed nearby to ask directions. Leaving their aircraft, the crew soon discovered that they were at Chalandry, near Laon on the enemy side of the lines. Attempting to reboard the bomber, Vereker was hauled down the ladder by a member of a German patrol and captured with his crew. There was no time to destroy the aircraft, and Vereker refused to fly it to a German base. It was dismantled and taken by road to Johannisthal, where it was re-assembled, examined, and test flown by several German pilots, allegedly including Manfred von Richthofen, who is said to have taken it to an altitude of 10,000 feet.

Despite this accidental 'presentation' of Britain's latest bomber to the Germans, it was quickly lost in a crash due to incorrectly rigged aileron cables, but not before it had been demonstrated to Kaiser Wilhelm.

The first O/100 operations were carried out in daylight, but following the loss of one brought down in the sea, sorties were switched to night. The 5th Wing, based at Dunkirk, operated O/100s against Bruges, Ostend, and Zeebrugge, and the 3rd Wing, based in Luxeuil, eastern France, flew O/100s against the industrial regions of the Saar. These night missions were at first by single aircraft due to an initial shortage of them, but a typical later operation was that of the night of 24/25 October 1917, when nine O/100s flew in a mass attack with an escort of sixteen F.E.s from Ochey.

The bomb load of the O/100 was originally intended to be made up of sixteen 112-pounders, but later changes were suggested to enable loads of up to four thousand pounds to be carried, dependent on the engines fitted. It was this ability to carry a heavy load, coupled with reliable engines capable of ensuring long-distance flights, that resulted in the O/100 being used for one of World War I's most spectacular sorties.

At the end of 1916, Squadron Commander Kenneth S. Savory, R.N. conceived a mission that was simple in its audacity, being nothing less than a bombing attack on the powerful German battle cruiser *Goeben* then in harbor at Stenia Bay, Turkey, where it was a threat to Russian vessels in the Black Sea as well as those of the western Allies in the Aegean. However, the mission called for a flight of nearly 2,000 miles from Manston in Kent to the Greek island of Mudros.

O/100 number 3124 was selected for the task. The extensive preparations required meant that it was 23 May 1917 before Savory and his crew were ready to depart on the first leg of the journey, which had been divided into two-hundred-mile (322 km) segments. The last segment was through mountainous country, for which only poor maps existed, and these had not been completed until the end of the first week in June.

Early O/100 serial number 1458 seen after delivery to No.3 Wing, RNAS, at Manston, Kent. The unusual roundels on its fuselage and wings anticipate the RAF markings of some twenty years later, although the outer rings here are white.

By now the original idea of a torpedo attack on *Goeben* had been dropped in favor of using 112-pound (51 kg) bombs. The attack was timed for 3 July, but had to be cancelled when the aircraft's engines overheated. The mission was rescheduled for 5 July, but this also had to be cancelled when burst tires made takeoff impossible. Bad weather three days later also forced a cancellation, but the weather improved on the following day, and Savory took off at 8:47 p.m., reaching the target five minutes before midnight.

The enemy was completely taken by surprise when the first salvo was dropped from an altitude of eight hundred feet (244 m) and started a fire. The next salvo scored a direct hit on the vessel. With eight bombs gone, Savory then took 3124 over the nearby Turkish War Office, claiming to have hit this from an altitude of 1,300 feet (396 m), aided by the light of the fire he had caused during his thirty-five minute stay over the target.

The O/100 afterwards remained at Mudros, where its maintenance proved to be a problem due to a lack of spare parts. On 30 September it was used in an attempted bombing attack on the railroad stations at Haydarpasa, but was forced down in the sea, probably by engine trouble. The three crewmen aboard, Lieutenants Wise, Aird, and Alcock, were taken prisoner. Lieutenant Alcock would later gain fame by flying across the Atlantic with Arthur Whitten Brown in a Vickers Vimy.

During its service use, the O/100 underwent a number of modifications, including revisions to the ailerons, horizontal stabilizer, and elevators, and the adoption of a simpler landing gear. In addition, the engine nacelles were shortened and the fuel tanks they formerly contained were repositioned in the fuselage. All these changes were to justify a new designation: the Handley Page O/400. (▶ 14)

▼ **The first prototype O/100, 1455 is seen here after modification to production standard. The serial number is carried on the extreme end of the fuselage in white, although the roundels are yet to be reduced to the standard smaller diameter.**

▲ **A prototype HP O/100, with experimental mass balances on its elevators, next to a Bristol Type 'C' single-seat scout.**

Early production model HP O/100 number 1463, which landed behind enemy lines on 1 January 1917 due to a faulty compass, is seen being examined after capture.

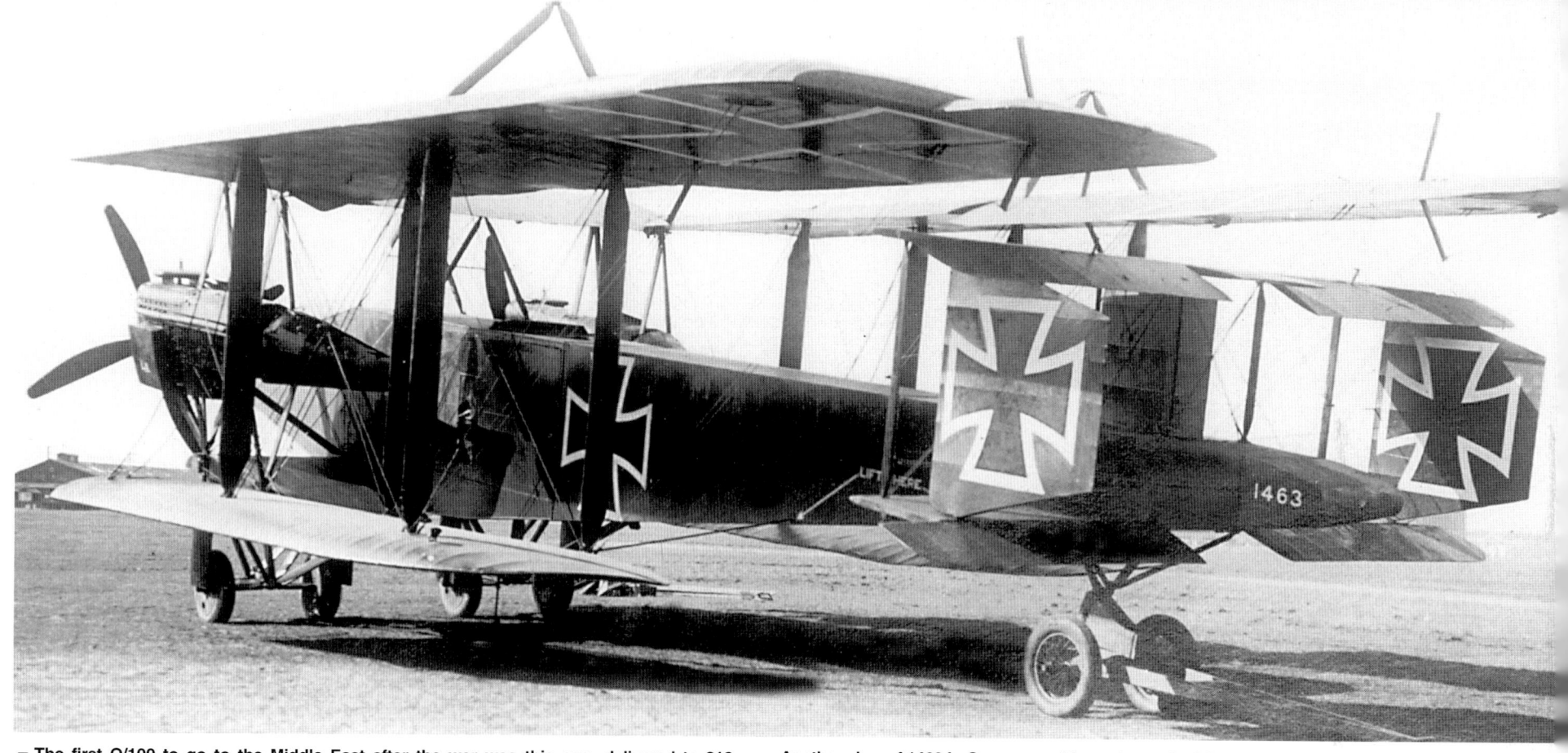

▼ The first O/100 to go to the Middle East after the war was this one, delivered to 216 Squadron, RAF, at Heliopolis, Egypt, in 1920. The squadron had earlier flown O/100 1459, the first in France.

▲ Another view of 1463 in German markings shows the PC10 upper surface finish still intact as indicated by the serial number on the rear fuselage.

Tail Variations

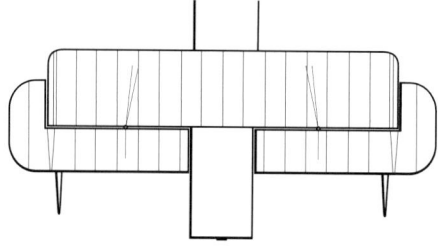

◀ Horizontal stabilizer and elevators on O/100 first and second prototypes (serial numbers 1455 and 1456 respectively).

▶ Modified horizontal stabilizer and elevators on O/100 production aircraft (serial number 1457 and subsequent).

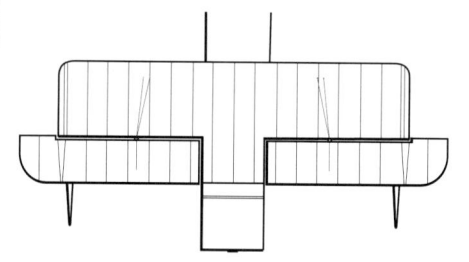

9

Handley Page O/100

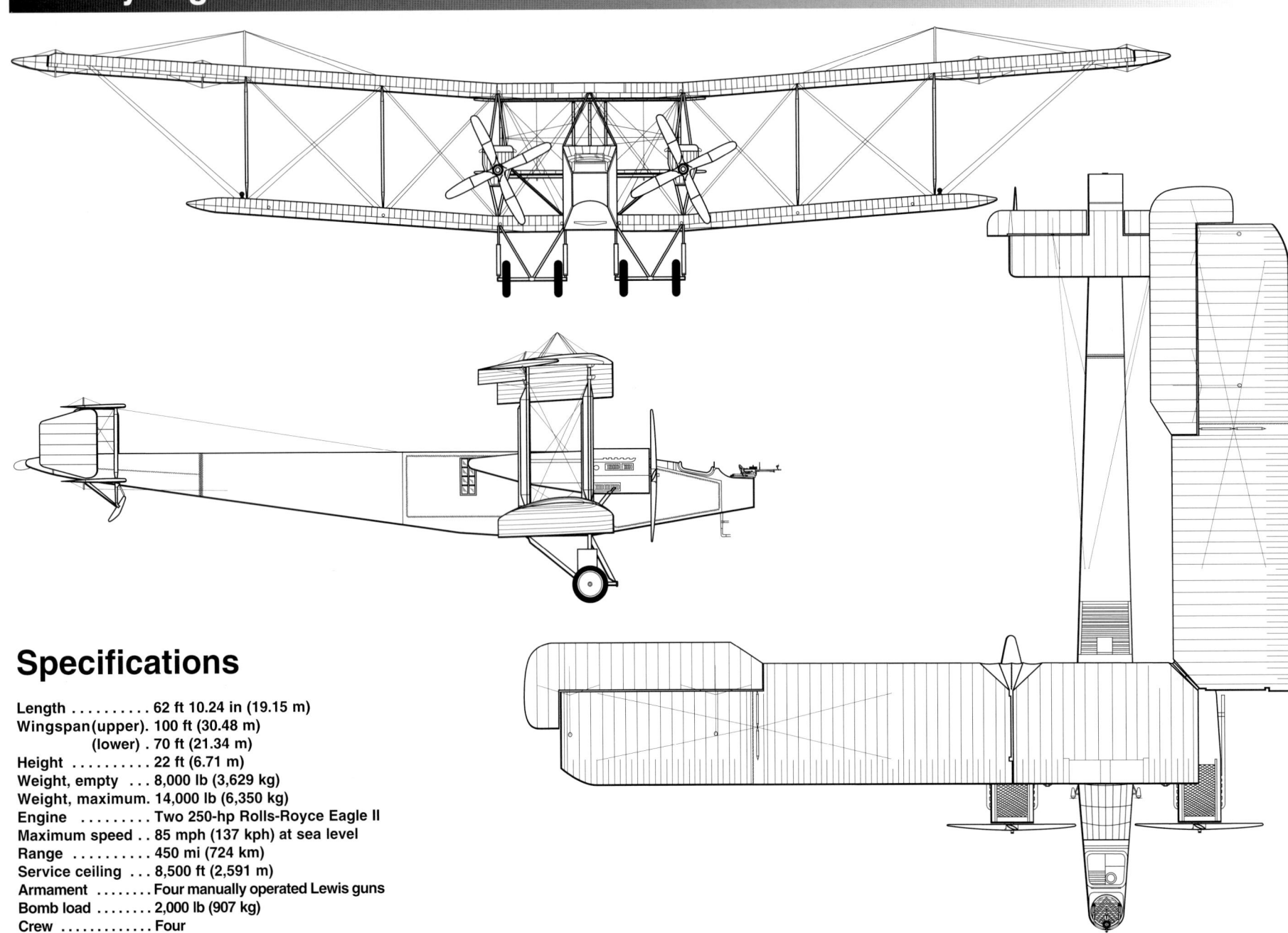

Specifications

Length .... 62 ft 10.24 in (19.15 m)
Wingspan (upper). 100 ft (30.48 m)
         (lower) . 70 ft (21.34 m)
Height .... 22 ft (6.71 m)
Weight, empty ... 8,000 lb (3,629 kg)
Weight, maximum. 14,000 lb (6,350 kg)
Engine .... Two 250-hp Rolls-Royce Eagle II
Maximum speed .. 85 mph (137 kph) at sea level
Range .... 450 mi (724 km)
Service ceiling ... 8,500 ft (2,591 m)
Armament .... Four manually operated Lewis guns
Bomb load .... 2,000 lb (907 kg)
Crew .... Four

Internal view of a Handley Page O/100 looking forward, showing the heavily wire-braced wooden structure of the period.

▲ A 320-horsepower Sunbeam 'Cossack' engine on a mobile test rig. Engines of this type were fitted to six O/100s, a twenty-hour flight test program being planned with them.

▲ A side view of Sunbeam 'Cossack' engine number 3123 on its test stand. This particular example had skirtless pistons and an improved exhaust manifold.

▼ One of the six Cossack-powered O/100s, B9446 is seen here with a group of Australian Flying Corps personnel at Halton, Buckinghamshire.

Landing Gear

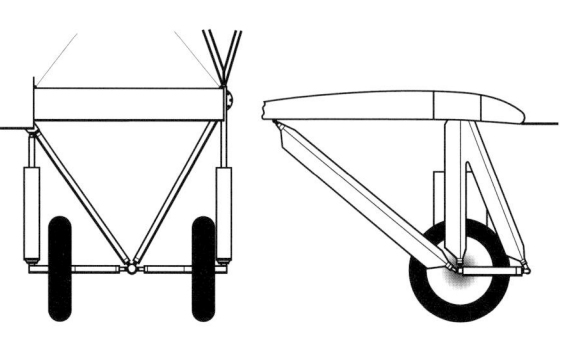

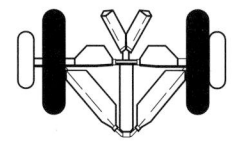

Port landing gear unit shown.

RNAS O/100 3124 lands on the Greek island of Mudros in 1917 after bombing the German battle cruiser *Goeben* on its flight from Britain. Its later bombing of Constantinople was the first intercontinental air attack in history.

Handley Page O/400

The new O/400 had little to distinguish it externally from the O/100 from which it had been developed, apart from the shortened engine nacelles made possible by the relocation of the fuel tanks to the fuselage. Changes included a new electrical system, a revised fuel system, propeller rotation in the same direction, a slightly offset vertical stabilizer, and enlarged radiators.

The first of the aircraft embodying these features was issued to the RNAS, chiefly to be used to combat operations by U-boats, then a serious threat to British overseas supplies. No. 16 (Naval) Squadron meanwhile began operations against such enemy industrial targets as Coblenz, Conflans, Mannheim, and Saarbrucken, and by the fall of 1918, the unit, now designated 216 Squadron, had been augmented by a number of O/400s taken from other squadrons. A typical mission was that of the night of 25/26 August 1918 by No. 215 Squadron, when factories at Mannheim were attacked from low level and then thoroughly strafed by the gunners working from the aircraft's three defensive positions.

At first these strategic attacks were conducted by pairs of O/400s. The usual bomb load for such operations consisted of twelve 112-pound (247 kg) bombs per aircraft. However, depending on the distance from the target, a maximum of eighteen 112-pounders could be carried (sixteen internally and a pair externally under the fuselage), or an equivalent total weight of larger bombs exceeding 500 pounds (1103 kg) each. Whatever their weight, all bombs carried internally were suspended by their noses and released electrically by a system which enabled preselecting the salvo size, whether single bombs or groups of four. The bombs were released through spring-loaded doors, which were opened by the weight of the bombs and immediately closed afterwards.

Only one O/400 saw operational use outside France. It was flown from the British Isles to Palestine by Brigadier-General A. E. Borton and Major A. S. C. Maclaren in July 1918 for the purpose of bombing the enemy's air base in the Der'a region, a base which was a threat to the work of Colonel T. E. Lawrence (better known as "Lawrence of Arabia"). On its outward journey, the bomber was used as a transport, bringing mail as well as a ton of gasoline and oil for the Bristol F.2b and de Havilland D.H.9 placed at Lawrence's disposal. This aircraft was eventually delivered to No.1 Squadron, Australian Flying Corps (No. 67 Squadron, RAF, until 5 February) in time to make a successful bombing attack on the Turkish general headquarters' telegraph and telephone exchange immediately before the launching of Allenby's offensive.

About four hundred of these important bombers were delivered before the Armistice from a total of seven hundred ordered. However, it was Lawrence's Arabs at Umm-es-Surab that gave perhaps the best description of the O/400 when they saw for the first time the machine sent to support their cause and commented, "Indeed and at last, they have sent us THE aeroplane!" By the standards of the time, they were right.

(▶▶ 23)

A picture taken with a fixed camera looking to the rear from the front cockpit. There are two figures in the dorsal gunner's position, the one on the left is adjusting rimless goggles. Pipework on the center-section struts connects with the two cylindrical 130 gallon fuel tanks beneath.

Handley Page O/400 C9681, which achieved the first England-to-Egypt flight in August 1918, at Aboukir. Crew, left to right, are Major A. S. C. Maclaren, Sergeant Goldfinch, Air Mechanic Francis, and Brigadier A. E. Borton. The flight later continued to Delhi, reached on 12 December. The notice behind reads "KEEP CLEAR OF THE PROPELLERS."

◀ An O/400 of No. 97 Squadron, seen here at Stonehenge in 1918, shows the way in which its wings could fold back in order to save space.

▶ Another O/400 with folded wings reveals details of the wing roots as well as the engine nacelle.

▸ Handley Page O/400 F314 is seen here at No. 14 Aircraft Acceptance Park before issue to an RAF squadron or going into storage. It was a late production model, built by the Birmingham Carriage Company, and might not have been delivered until as late as 1920. The nose gunner's position has twin Lewis guns.

◂ O/400 D8326 was known as the 'Silver Star' from its color scheme. It is seen here at RAF Hendon, North London, when flown by No.1 (Communications) Squadron. The fuselage band is believed to be Roundel Blue with red edges. The small roundel on the rudder is unusual.

Handley Page O/400

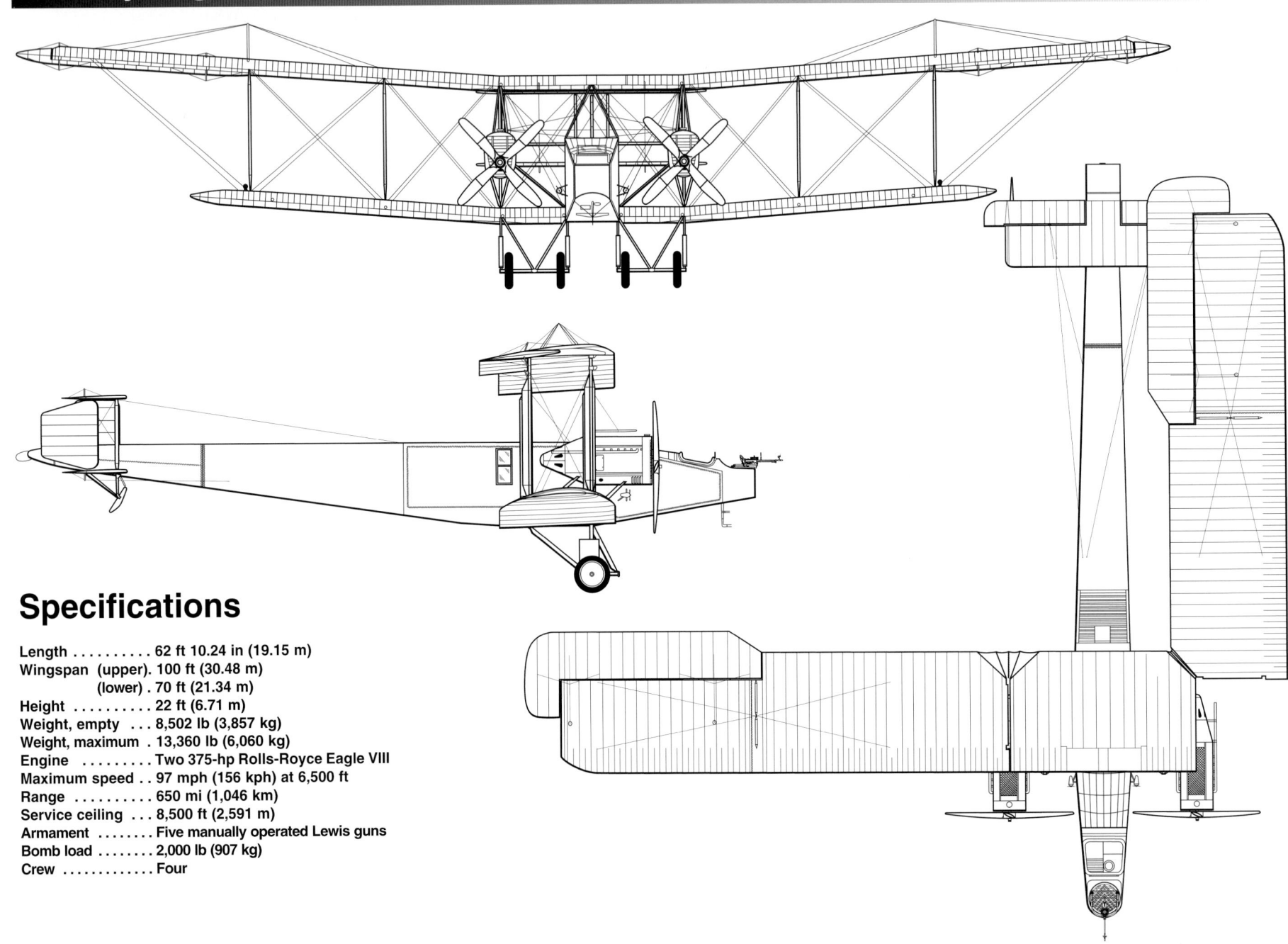

Specifications

Length . . . . 62 ft 10.24 in (19.15 m)
Wingspan (upper). 100 ft (30.48 m)
　　　　　(lower) . 70 ft (21.34 m)
Height . . . . 22 ft (6.71 m)
Weight, empty . . . 8,502 lb (3,857 kg)
Weight, maximum . 13,360 lb (6,060 kg)
Engine . . . . Two 375-hp Rolls-Royce Eagle VIII
Maximum speed . . 97 mph (156 kph) at 6,500 ft
Range . . . . 650 mi (1,046 km)
Service ceiling . . . 8,500 ft (2,591 m)
Armament . . . . Five manually operated Lewis guns
Bomb load . . . . 2,000 lb (907 kg)
Crew . . . . Four

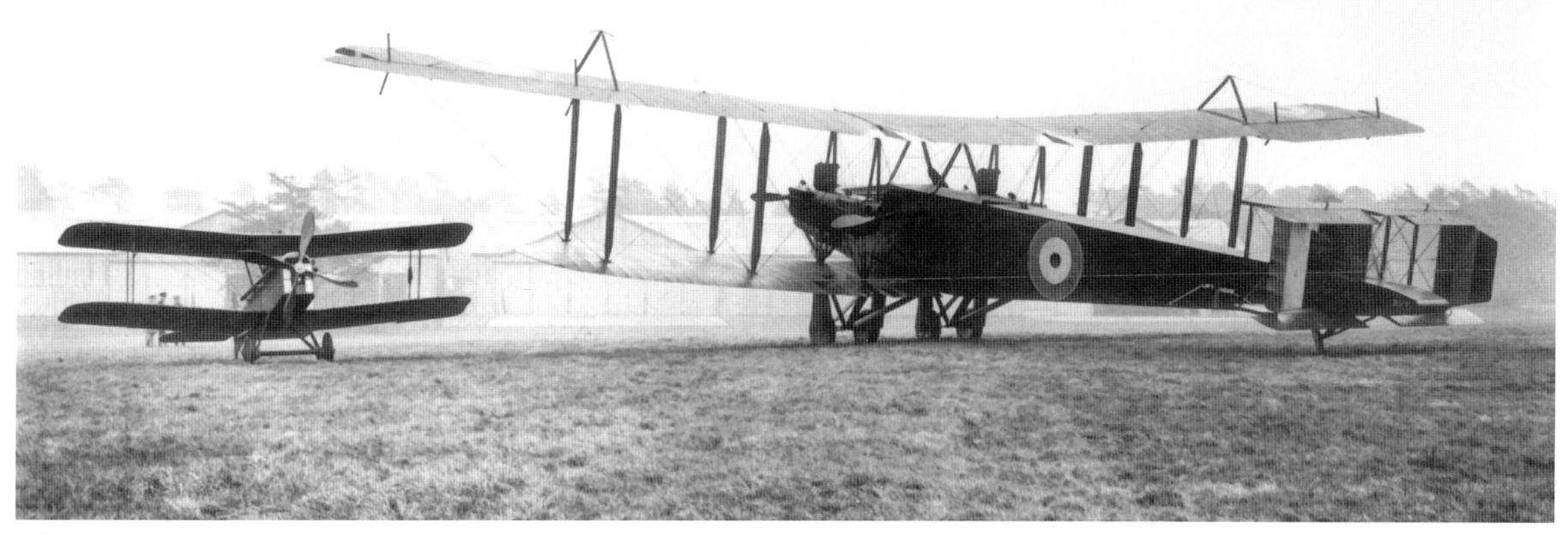

▲ Seen here at Farnborough, Hampshire, on 8 February 1918 in company with an S.E.5A, O/100 3117 was tested with both Sunbeam and Hispano engines after having been modified with four 200-horsepower Hispano Suiza 'push-pull' engines in November 1917 as a test installation for the Handley Page V-1500.

▼ Photographed at Portholme in August 1918, O/400 D9702 was a late production aircraft of a batch ordered from Clayton and Shuttleworth, the majority of which were cancelled. It was powered by a pair of Sunbeam Maori engines.

▲ The large serial number on the side of this O/400 indicates that it was originally a bomber converted for use as an airliner by Handley Page Transport Ltd., with its former service serial number temporarily used as a registration. It later became fully civilianized as G-EAAW. It was withdrawn from use on 10 January 1923.

▼ This view of an O/400 emphasizes several features of the type, including the shorter engine nacelles, made possible by the moving of the fuel tanks from the rear of the nacelles into the fuselage. The rectangular tail flash instead of rudder stripes also was common to the O/400.

▼ A typical tail 'trolley,' used to assist crew in maneuvering the O/400 on the ground.

An unidentified Handley page O/400 in what appears to be a clear dope finish. Note the small roundel on the underside of the upper wingtip.

▲ O/400 D5426 was on the strength of 115 Squadron, RAF, which operated the type as part of the Independent Air Force from July 1918 until its disbanding in 1919. The squadron's first raid using the O/400 was against Metz-Sablon on 16/17 December, when four tons of bombs were dropped. Night handling markings appear on the rear fuselage.

▼ The components of this O/400 were manufactured by No.1 National Aircraft Factory at Waddon, near Croydon, Surrey, but were sent to Cricklewood, North West London, for assembly by United States personnel. The dorsal bulge aft of the cockpit was a long-range fuel tank.

▲ The nose gunner of an H.P. O/400 poses in his gun ring at Cressy on 27 September 1918. Beneath his Lewis gun is an early drift sight, while below the nose is the pitot head. Behind is a Bessoneau canvas hangar.

American 'H-Pip' O/400s

In June 1917, shortly after the United States entered World War I, drawings of the Handley Page O/400 had been forwarded to McCook Field for examination by Army officials. In 1918 the aircraft was selected for construction in the U.S., and 'H-Pip,' the British slang term for the aircraft based on the phonetic alphabet of the time, was slowly absorbed into American speech.

American O/400s were to be powered, not by the standard Rolls-Royce Eagle VIII engines of the British examples, but a pair of Liberty 12-Ns. Modifications devised by the Engineering Division of the U.S. Signal Corps took advantage of the strength of the Handley Page airframe to take the new Liberty engines.

To aid the American production effort, a sample airframe was sent to McCook Field in January 1918. This aircraft was B9449, one of six O/100s powered by 320-horsepower Sunbeam Cossack engines, with the additional or different components which made it an O/400 painted red to aid identification. An order for five hundred O/400s was quickly placed with the Standard Aircraft Corporation, and a further thousand were ordered in August 1918 to equip thirty U.S. Army squadrons based in Europe, but the day before production was due to commence, these orders were cancelled due to the swift changes in the war situation.

Apart from the different engines, American Handley Pages also differed from their British counterparts in using cotton fabric instead of linen, despite the fact that the cotton had to be covered with cellulose acetate, which was in short supply, rather than the more readily available nitrate dope. It was in cellulose acetate-doped cotton that the first Standard-built O/400 was delivered, with the appropriate name 'Langley' on its side and crossed U.S. and British national flags painted on its nose. However, this clear dope finish did not last long, as it was soon replaced by one of olive drab with tricolor rudder stripes and red and blue roundels, although the flag decoration was retained. American O/400s also had a slightly different nose gunner's position, which was higher than that of British examples, with a pair of Marlin .30-caliber machine guns on a linked Scarff mounting instead of the Lewis guns of the British aircraft.

United States interest in the O/400 also extended to plans to assemble a number of aircraft in Britain from parts shipped from the U.S. One hundred sets of parts were shipped for assembly by National Aircraft Factory No.1 at Waddon, Surrey, but the exact number completed is unknown. F5349 was assembled by U.S. Air Service personnel at Ford Junction (now Ford) in Sussex during October 1918 and went to Cricklewood for flight tests early in the following year — the only British-built O/400 to have Liberty engines.

In the United States, three O/400s were delivered, one known to have had the raised nose gunner's position, and twenty others, with British-type noses, were immediately placed in storage. Of these, seven were refurbished in 1920 to take part in General Billy Mitchell's bombing trials, dropping externally carried 2,000-pound (907 kg) and 4,000-pound (1,814 kg) bombs on captured German warships in Chesapeake Bay.

A total of 107 American O/400s are believed to have been completed; the majority went straight into storage.

(▶ 27)

▲ O/400 B8811 of 207 Squadron, RAF, flies over German territory in May 1919. The widely spaced codes on the fuselage were 'A•2,' divided by the side roundel. Strong top lighting here gives an illusion of a light finish, but the finish was standard P.C.10 upper surfaces.

▶ A Handley Page O/400 of 207 Squadron, Independent Air Force, is towed out by a Clayton and Shuttleworth tractor in August 1918. A drift sight is fitted to the nose. The caps of the personnel confirm that the unit was originally a Royal Naval Air Service squadron.

▲ Apart from its United States national markings under the lower wings, little is known about this O/400, but it may be one of the 15,000 ordered from the Standard Aircraft Corporation to be powered with 350-horsepower Liberty 12N engines. The first such machine was delivered in September 1918.

◄ American O/400 'Langley' seen here at Wright Field with red and white roundels under the upper wingtips. It was rebuilt from B9449, one of a batch of five aircraft of varying types which were assembled from salvaged parts and spares.

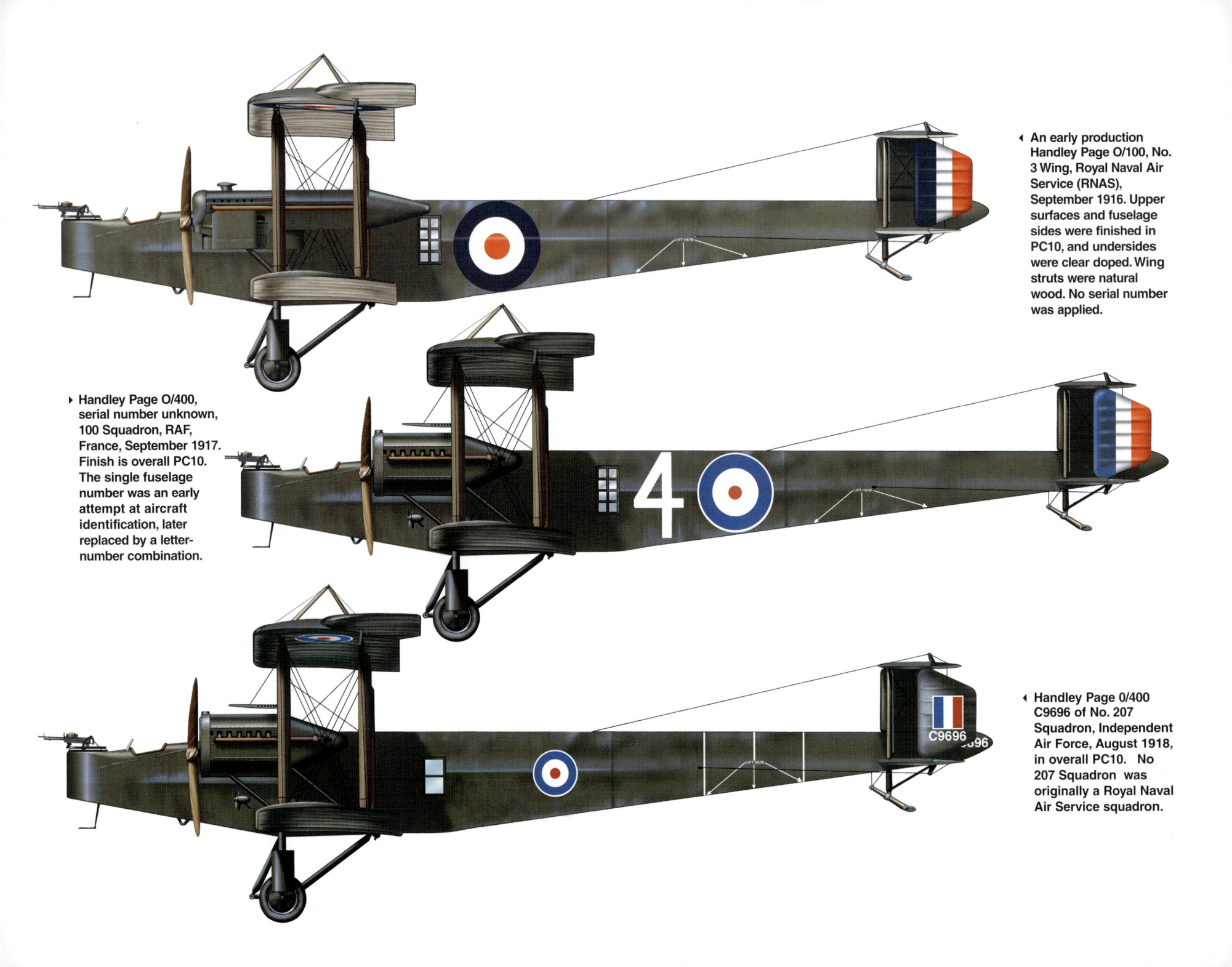

◀ An early production Handley Page O/100, No. 3 Wing, Royal Naval Air Service (RNAS), September 1916. Upper surfaces and fuselage sides were finished in PC10, and undersides were clear doped. Wing struts were natural wood. No serial number was applied.

▶ Handley Page O/400, serial number unknown, 100 Squadron, RAF, France, September 1917. Finish is overall PC10. The single fuselage number was an early attempt at aircraft identification, later replaced by a letter-number combination.

◀ Handley Page O/400 C9696 of No. 207 Squadron, Independent Air Force, August 1918, in overall PC10. No 207 Squadron was originally a Royal Naval Air Service squadron.

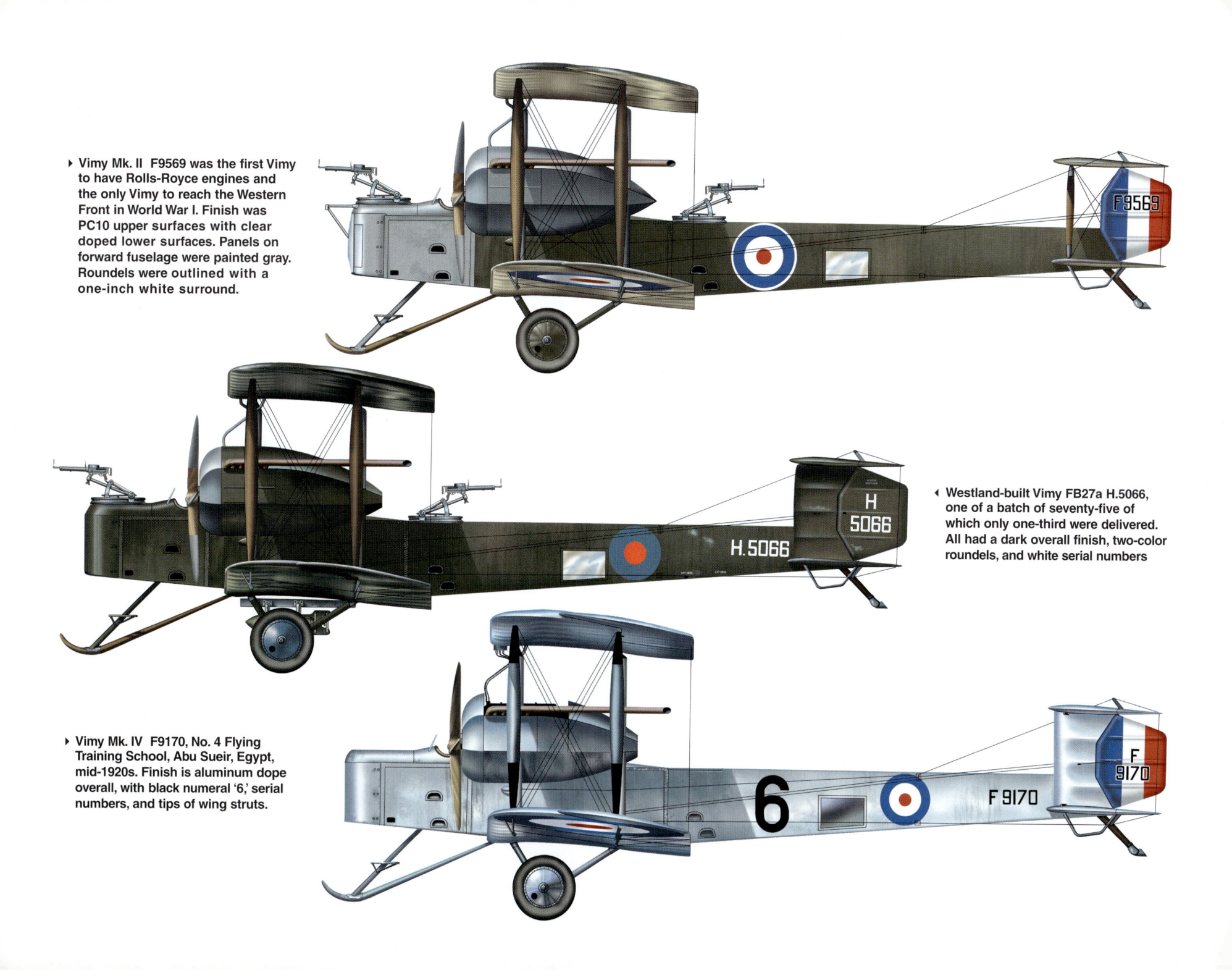

▸ Vimy Mk. II F9569 was the first Vimy to have Rolls-Royce engines and the only Vimy to reach the Western Front in World War I. Finish was PC10 upper surfaces with clear doped lower surfaces. Panels on forward fuselage were painted gray. Roundels were outlined with a one-inch white surround.

◂ Westland-built Vimy FB27a H.5066, one of a batch of seventy-five of which only one-third were delivered. All had a dark overall finish, two-color roundels, and white serial numbers

▸ Vimy Mk. IV F9170, No. 4 Flying Training School, Abu Sueir, Egypt, mid-1920s. Finish is aluminum dope overall, with black numeral '6,' serial numbers, and tips of wing struts.

Handley Page V/1500

The ultimate development of the Handley Page bombers of World War I was the gigantic V/1500, which had a wingspan of only some forty feet less than that of a Boeing 747, and pioneered the use of four engines in a tandem layout, with one tractor engine and one pusher engine in each of two nacelles. The existence of the V/1500, intended to attack Germany from Great Britain, was such a closely guarded military secret that the design work was undertaken by British technicians in Iceland, and the crews were specially picked men who had undergone a special course in navigating these huge aircraft. However, the late entry of the V/1500 into production meant that when the Armistice was signed in November 1918, only three were standing by ready for their first mission at 166 Squadron's base at Bircham Newton, Norfolk.

The first of these 'Super-Handleys,' as some called them at the time, made its initial flight in May 1918. A setback was to follow when it crashed in June and proved impossible to replace until the following October. Originally, a total of 225 were ordered, to be powered by two Rolls-Royce Condor engines. However, these powerplants were not ready in time, so four Rolls-Royce Eagles were substituted as had been done on the earlier O/400, a fact which emphasizes that there was nothing unconventional about the V/1500 except for its size and its fourteen-hour endurance.

That the V/1500 was the herald of a new strategic bombing policy is proven by the formation of a second RAF squadron to fly the type at the same time as No. 166, that being No.167, which was probably created at the same base as the former. It is doubtful, however, that 167 Squadron ever received any of the new bombers, as it was formed in the same month that saw the end of the war.

The war's end quickly resulted in the cancellation of a large number of aircraft production contracts that had been issued, and it may be that only about eight V/1500s were actually built. Some authorities claim that as many as thirty-three were delivered, although neither of the specialist squadrons were ever completely equipped with the type. The last V/1500 built, which first flew on 3 September 1919, differed from the main production version in being powered by Napier Lion engines.

Almost now forgotten is that the Handley-Page V/1500 was used in an unusual series of trials of potential new methods of aircraft armament. In 1918, one was used to test a three-inch mortar fired from the dorsal gun position. The shell, which arced up in a high parabola over the tail of the aircraft and burst 250 feet aft, most likely would have destroyed any interceptor on the bomber's tail. Another series of armament experiments using a V/1500 tested a rear gun turret.

The V/1500 found no postwar work, as the type was found to be too expensive to operate either in a commercial or military role in the peacetime economy. However the type's long-range capability did result in it being pressed into service for the first flight between England and India. The flight, under the command of Brigadier-General N. D. K. McEwen, was taken in easy stages via Rome, Malta, Cairo, and Baghdad between 13 December 1918 and 27 January 1919. The crew consisted of pilots Major A. S. MacLaren MC and Captain Robert Halley, plus three mechanics.

V/1500 F7140 was shipped to Newfoundland in 1919 to be prepared for an attempted crossing of the Atlantic, but this effort was abandoned when the Vickers Vimy flown by Alcock and Brown successfully accomplished the feat. The Handley Page was relegated to a program of demonstrations in Canada and the United States.

(▶ 31)

The long-distance Handley page V/1500 J1936, on what at the time was called "the Ipswitch-to-India flight," photographed in the early morning of Tuesday, 9 January 1919, near the Baghdad railroad station, which at the time was "just a shed on the Berlin to Mesopotamia rail line."

Handley Page V/1500

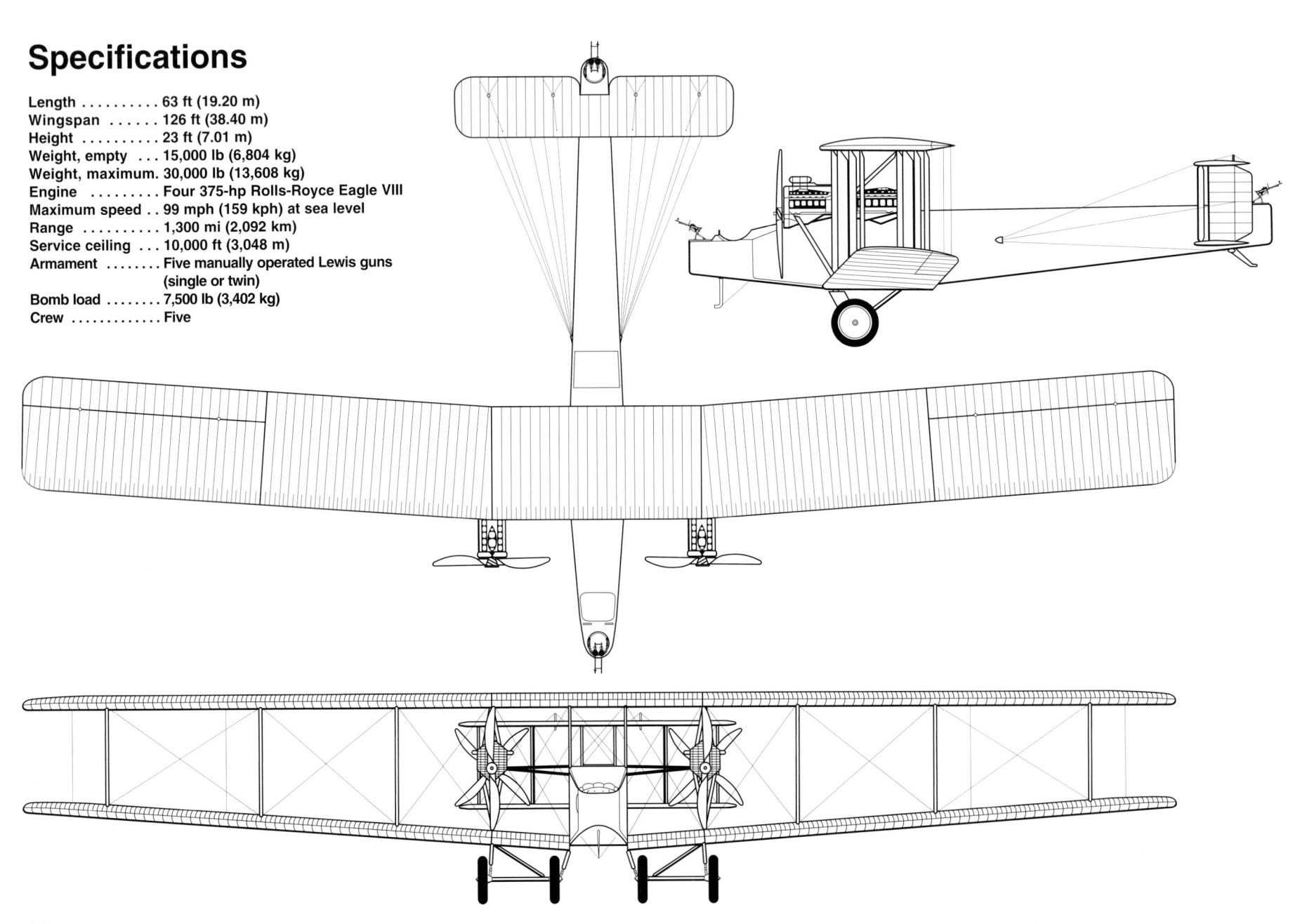

Specifications

- **Length** .... 63 ft (19.20 m)
- **Wingspan** ...... 126 ft (38.40 m)
- **Height** .... 23 ft (7.01 m)
- **Weight, empty** ... 15,000 lb (6,804 kg)
- **Weight, maximum** . 30,000 lb (13,608 kg)
- **Engine** .... Four 375-hp Rolls-Royce Eagle VIII
- **Maximum speed** .. 99 mph (159 kph) at sea level
- **Range** .... 1,300 mi (2,092 km)
- **Service ceiling** ... 10,000 ft (3,048 m)
- **Armament** .... Five manually operated Lewis guns (single or twin)
- **Bomb load** .... 7,500 lb (3,402 kg)
- **Crew** .... Five

▲ J1936 after landing. Before its arrival, the area, which had been a forward base for the Royal Army Medical Corps, was cleared by the Military Police. Landing at Ambala in the dusk with all its lights on, it "caused consternation among the natives."

▼ An early view of a Handley Page V/1500 which shows the 'push-pull' engine installation and emphasizes the massive proportions of the design when compared with the figures grouped under it. V/1500s were first known only as "Super-Handleys."

▲ The long-distance Handley Page V/1500 before its departure from England showing its name 'Old Carthusian' on the nose under the letters 'H.M.A.' (an abbreviation of 'His Majesty's Aeroplane').

▼ V/1500 J1936 at Ambala in March 1919. After its record-breaking long-distance flight, it was used to bomb Afghan rebels near Kabul in the following May. By this time the rectangular tail markings of earlier Handley Page bombers had been abandoned, to be replaced by conventional vertical stripes.

Vickers Vimy

Britain's second-generation heavy bombers tended to be smaller than their predecessors. They included such types as the de Havilland D.H.10, popularly called the 'Amiens,' and the Vickers Vimy. Neither of these was to see action in the First World War, although both were designed and the prototypes flown before the Armistice.

The first Vimy, B9952, made its first flight from Joyce Green, Kent, on 30 November 1917 after a design and construction period of only four months. This aircraft was powered by a pair of 200-horsepower Hispano Suiza engines housed in clumsy-looking rectangular nacelles. In its official trials at Martlesham Heath in January of the following year, the Vimy made a sensational debut when it lifted a load greater than that of the Handley Page O/400, an aircraft which had nearly twice the power.

Later modifications to B9952 included a change to a pair of 200-horsepower Salmson water-cooled radial engines, a modified tail unit, a transparent panel in the nose, and a plywood-covered forward fuselage. A second prototype, B9953, appeared in April 1918, this example having inversely tapered ailerons and 260-horsepower Sunbeam Maori engines which extended endurance by more than an hour. The third and final prototype, B9954, delivered in August 1918, was largely similar except for having two 300-horsepower Fiat engines, external bomb racks, and two alternative sets of wings, one with balanced ailerons. Few trials of this aircraft were carried out, as it was destroyed in a forced landing with live bombs aboard.

Now named 'Vimy' and described as a short-distance night bomber, the new aircraft was ordered in quantity from Vickers and a number of sub-contractors, including the Westland Aircraft organization. The production model, designated Mk. IV, had vertical stabilizers unlike the prototypes, and was powered by two 360-horsepower Rolls-Royce Eagle VIII engines. Plans to test a version powered by American 400-horsepower Liberty engines, allegedly for use by the U.S. Air Service, were abandoned when the only prototype was destroyed in an accidental fire.

Although the replacement prototype Vimy reached the RAF's Independent Air Force at Nancy by October 1918, the first production versions to enter RAF service were those which went to No. 58 Squadron during July of the following year, replacing its Handley Page O/400 in Egypt. These were followed in late 1921 by deliveries to Nos. 45 and 70 Squadrons, all these being described as capable of carrying a bomb load of 2,402 pounds (1,090 kg) — half the declared wartime capacity. At home, No.100 Squadron received the Vimy at Spittlegate during 1922, but was not completely re-equipped, only the Squadron's 'D' Flight flying the Vimys.

All together the Vimy equipped only nine RAF bomber squadrons, four of them in Egypt, plus No. 4 Flying Training School at Heliopolis. Many of the Vimys serving outside the United Kingdom presented an unfamiliar appearance operating without their cowlings in order to assist in engine cooling. The serial numbers of some rebuilt machines gradually acquired a letter "R" as a suffix to their sequence letter following reconstruction ('J657' became 'JR657,' for example).

Some units flying the Vimy in Egypt made use of an unusual navigational aid, a plowed ravine marking part of the 860-mile route between Cairo and Baghdad through inhospitable scorched terrain, 2,000 feet and more above sea level. This route was first instituted for air mail flights, but was later taken as part of a widening commercial network. Despite being marked out in 1921, parts of it were reported to still be visible in 1986.

Not all Vimys in RAF use were bombers. Among the small number otherwise employed were J7451, used for trials with smoke-producing apparatus at the Royal Aircraft Establishment, Farnborough, and one fitted with a 37 mm C.O.W. (Coventry Ordnance Works) shell-firing, semi-automatic gun. Others, such as F9161 and J7441, were used at RAF Henlow as parachute trainers, these being distinguished by tall and broad 'ladders' extending above the fuselage on the port side in line with the dorsal gunner's position.

The last Vimy bombers to see use were those of 502 Squadron at Aldergrove in Northern Ireland, which did not relinquish them until summer 1928 in favor of the new Handley Page Hyderabad. From 1925 until 1929 some eighty Vimys were refitted with either Bristol Jupiter or Armstrong Siddeley Jaguar radial engines and served at parachute and flying training establishments. The very last Vimys used by the RAF must have been those which, nineteen years later, were used to give practice to Army searchlight trainees immediately before the outbreak of World War II.

▼ The first prototype Vickers Vimy, B9952, which made its maiden flight on 30 November 1917, is seen here at Martlesham Heath where it arrived for trials on 10 January 1918. By this time the radiators had been enlarged and the upright exhaust stacks replaced by horizontal pipes.

▼ B9954, the last of three Vickers Vimy prototypes, on 15 August 1918, the day it arrived at Martlesham Heath. This particular aircraft had a slightly modified nose and was powered by Fiat engines. It was used mainly for propeller trials. It crashed twenty-seven days later and was destroyed when its bomb load exploded.

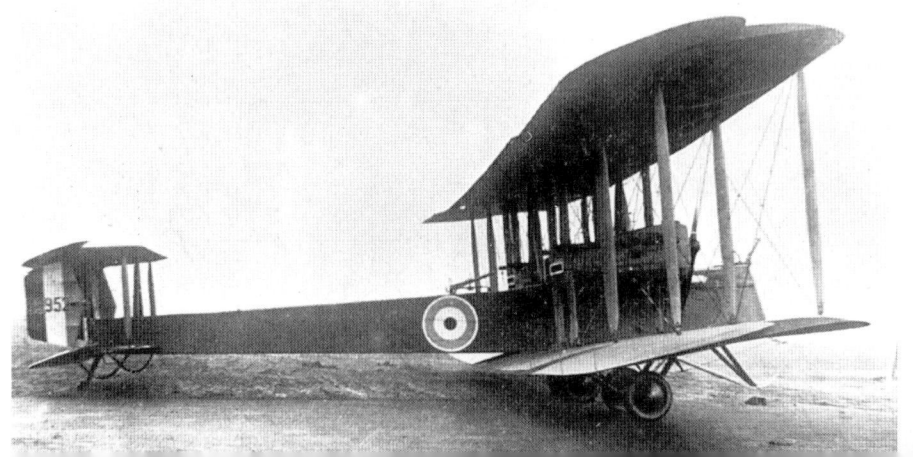

Vickers Vimy IV

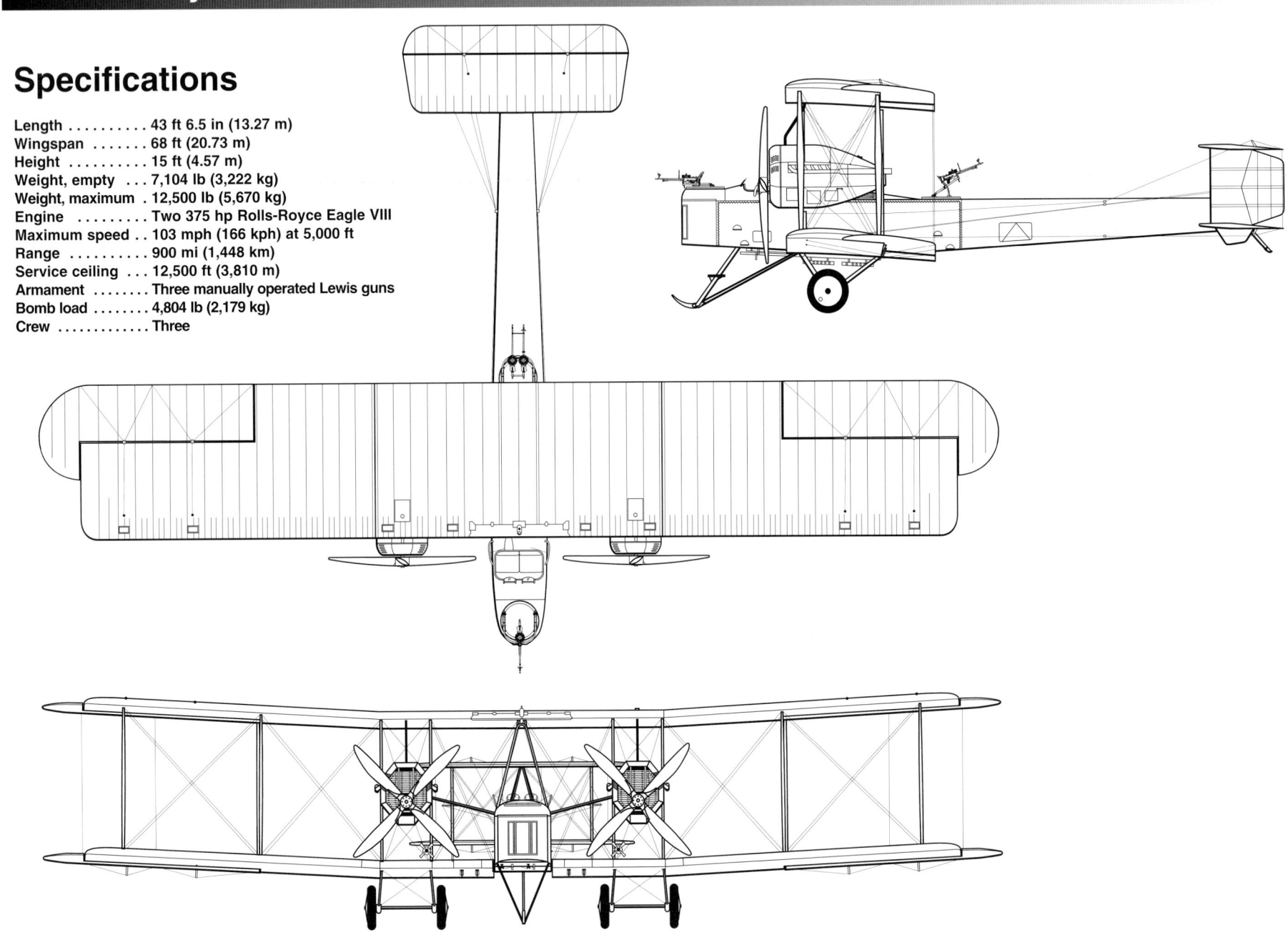

Specifications

Length . . . . 43 ft 6.5 in (13.27 m)
Wingspan . . . . 68 ft (20.73 m)
Height . . . . 15 ft (4.57 m)
Weight, empty . . . 7,104 lb (3,222 kg)
Weight, maximum . 12,500 lb (5,670 kg)
Engine . . . . Two 375 hp Rolls-Royce Eagle VIII
Maximum speed . . 103 mph (166 kph) at 5,000 ft
Range . . . . 900 mi (1,448 km)
Service ceiling . . . 12,500 ft (3,810 m)
Armament . . . . Three manually operated Lewis guns
Bomb load . . . . 4,804 lb (2,179 kg)
Crew . . . . Three

▲ No.4 Flying Training School flew F9170, one of a batch of a hundred originally ordered but only half delivered due to postwar economies. The tips of the wing struts, like the figure '6' on the fuselage side, were black. F9170 by this time had been converted to dual control.

▲ Vimy IV F8631, from the same production batch as F8596 (below), was delivered in an entirely aluminum dope scheme, a finish briefly adopted for night-bombers. It was first issued to the newly re-formed No. 9 Squadron in 1924 and later to No. 7 Squadron before being sent overseas to No. 4 Flying Training School.

▼ F8596 was the first of a batch of fifty Vickers Vimys built at the Weybridge, Surrey, works of the parent company. The original order had specified either Fiat or B.H.P. engines, but the majority was finally fitted with Rolls-Royce Eagles. The fins of this aircraft appear to have been removed.

Seen here in aluminum dope finish, Vimy IV F9158 was used for trials to investigate the use of oleo undercarriage legs and for braking tests. F9186 from the same production batch was used in ditching trials in 1920.

The post-1918 economies expected of the armed forces not only resulted in production cutbacks but also imposed stringent thrift at the squadron level, resulting in many aircraft receiving temporary repairs to their fabric rather than a complete recovering. This Vimy came from the same production batch as that in the preceding photograph.

▲ Vimy H5068 was built by the Westland Aircraft Company of Yeovil, Somerset, one of an order of seventy-five, of which only a third was delivered. All had dark finishes, two-color roundels, and white serial numbers. Several were rebuilt, rebuilt aircraft being indicated by the addition of a 'R' to the serial. H5068 became HR5068 after rebuilding.

▼ Another Westland-built Vimy IV was H5089 '1.' It flew with 216 Squadron RAF from Kantara, Egypt, in 1922. H5089 later became HR5089 after rebuilding.

▲ To judge from the faded two-color roundel, which has been made from one originally having three colors, F8618 'B' spent some time in the Middle East. A Westland-built machine similar to this was once looped by test pilot Squadron Leader 'Rollo' A. de Haga Haig, AFC.

▼ The Air Officer Commanding, Middle East, inspects No.4 Flying Training School, Abu Suir, Egypt, which has its aluminum-doped Vickers Vimys drawn up outside the school sheds.

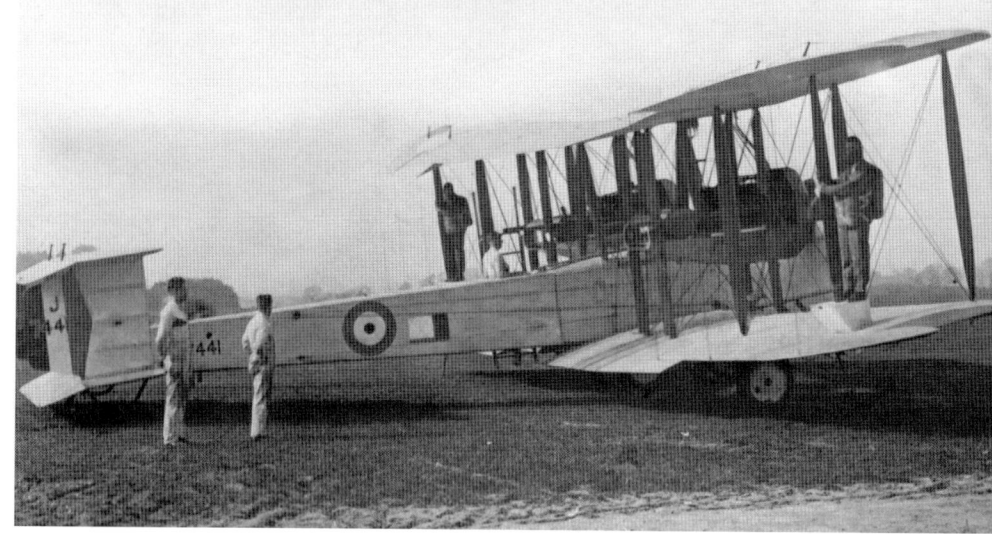

▲ In addition to bomber and dual-control versions of the Vickers Vimy, there existed those modified for parachute training, such as J7441 seen here. This was one of a small order for fifteen placed in June 1924. Trainees jumped from miniature platforms built on the lower wings, aft of the outboard rear wing struts. Others were JR7444 and JR7454.

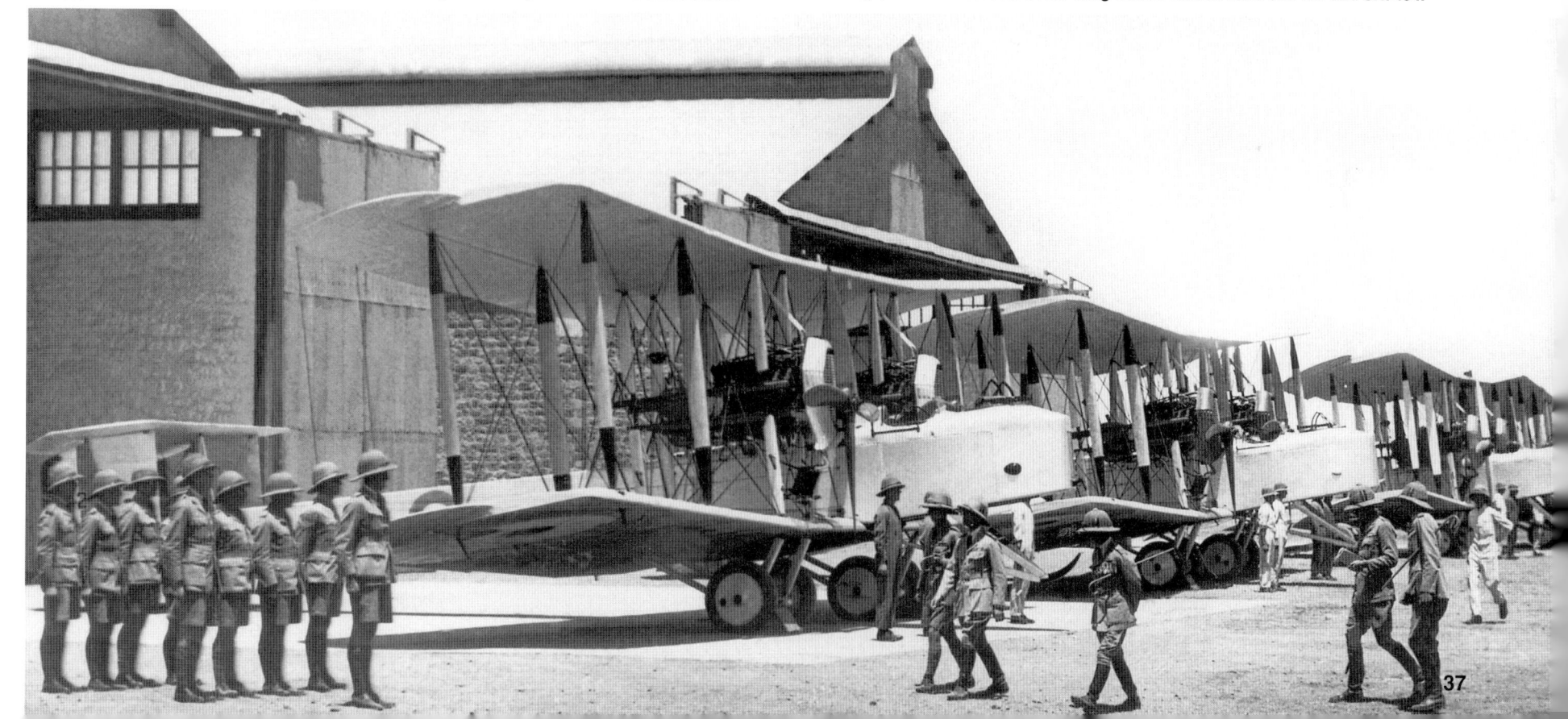

Civilian Use

As bombers must be able to carry a heavy load and must have a comparatively long range, the postwar adaptation of surplus O/400s for use as passenger transports was only natural. Such conversions were carried out not only in England, but also in every other country that had developed such military aircraft. France, for example, based her Goliath airliners on the Farman FF.60 prototype of 1918, while the later Liore et Olivier LeO 21 was evolved from the LeO 12 bomber, and Germany adapted the A.E.G. G.V. for use as an airliner.

The first Handley Page airliners were little more that O/400s fitted with seats. Fourteen of these appeared on the civilian market by January 1920; all had been given RAF serial numbers, but none had been issued to a squadron.

Seven other O/400s were specially adapted by moving the fuselage fuel tanks into the rear of the engine nacelles, transferring oil tanks to the upper wing, cutting windows in the sides, and fitting seats for fourteen passengers. These aircraft were at first designated H.P. O/700, later abbreviated to O/7. Many of these attracted the attention of China, then establishing an internal airline network.

The O/7s were superseded by Handley Page O/10s, which retained their internal fuel tanks, but were fitted with two extra passenger seats in the former nose gunner's position. These were quickly followed by O/11s, which, except for having three passenger seats, were used to carry cargo. One O/11 was purchased by the Thakur Sahib of the Indian Princely State of Morvi and was gorgeously fitted inside.

The Vickers Vimy also proved to be adaptable to civilian use. Probably the best known of these was the unregistered aircraft used by Alcock and Brown in 1919 to fly across the Atlantic for the first time. Others were G-EAOU, in which brothers Ross and Keith Smith flew to Australia in 1919, and G-UABA, in which Lieutenant Colonel Pierre van Ryneveld and Major Quintin Brand attempted to fly from Cairo to Cape Town in 1920.

Most of these civilianized Vimys were in effect hybrids. Only three true Vimy IVs, all of them originally constructed as RAF bombers, were to bear British civilian registrations. These were: G-EAAR, which carried its constructor's number ('C-105') instead of its allocated registration markings during a career that ran only from May 1919 to May 1920; G-EAOL, formerly 'F8625,' which was sold to Spain in 1920; and Ross and Keith Smith's G-EAOU, formerly 'F8630,' which is currently preserved in Australia.

◄ **Another civilian Vimy, Alcock and Brown's transatlantic aircraft gets airborne from Lester's Field, Newfoundland, on 14 June 1919. Sixteen hours and twenty-eight minutes later it landed in Ireland after a journey of 1,890 miles.**

▶ **The Atlantic-crossing Vimy, heavy with fuel, slowly climbs away at 1300 hours local time on 14 June 1919, Alcock at the controls and Brown navigating.**

▲ Pioneer record-breakers Ross and Keith Smith with their crewmen, Sergeants J. W. Bennett and W. H. Shiers, pose in front of a standard Vimy. All military equipment was removed from their long-distance aircraft.

▲ Another postwar event which drew public attention to the Vickers Vimy was the flight from London, England, to Australia by brothers Captain Ross Smith and Lieutenant Keith Smith in civilian Vimy G-EAOU, November-December 1919.

▲ A civilianized Vickers Vimy at Beddington Aerodrome, Surrey. The aircraft is G-EAOL (formerly F8625), which first flew on 20 September 1919 and was used as a sales demonstrator in Spain, where it was finally sold about 1920. Beddington Aerodrome was later enlarged to become Croydon Airport.

▼ Ex-RAF O/400 C9699 carries its new British civil registration G-EASL shortly after its first use as a passenger aircraft on 23 June 1920 by the Handley Page Transport Company. The marking 'HP30' on the rear fuselage was a conversion number, not a type designation. The aircraft was withdrawn from civilian use in April 1921.

Another ex-O/400 bomber was D.8350, carrying its former RAF serial number as a temporary civil registration. The letter 'G' on the tail signified that it was British. Redesignated an HP-16, it was operated by the Handley Page Transport Company until its withdrawal in August 1920, by then having been named 'Vulture.'

▲ The first Handley Page O/400 converted as a civil airliner was F5414, seen here in its bomber form. It became G-EAAF on 1 May 1919 and was redesignated a Type O/7 in August. It was withdrawn from use in 1923.

▼ Bearing the marking 'HP-1,' an early and experimental attempt at aircraft identification, an O/7 of Handley Page Transport awaits its passengers. This particular aircraft was also registered as K-162, and later, G-EAGN.

Handley Page O/10 G-EATK had been O/400 J2262 when owned by the RAF. From 1920 to 1922, it operated as a civil airliner from Croydon, Surrey. It is seen here after being refitted with Jupiter engines.

G-EATG was an HP O/10 converted from O/400 D4618 and given the factory number 'HP-37.' It began operations with Handley Page Transport on 23 June 1920 only to be scrapped two years later.

Construction Details

The Handley Page aircraft generally were of similar construction, with wire-braced wooden fuselages, wings, and tail surfaces, all largely covered in fabric. Some exterior portions were covered by three-ply wooden panels. The HP O/400, for example, had plywood covering around the nose gunner's compartment and the extreme tip of the rear fuselage. Sheet metal surrounded the cockpit, and aft of this, the 'turtle deck' was plywood-covered back to a point in line with the main wing spars. A rectangular vertical stabilizer was fixed to the center of the upper surface of the rear fuselage between the twin rudders. Fuselage windows were made of clear Pyralin, a celluloid plastic.

The O/100 initially had armor protection for a number of areas, but after the first trials, most of the armor was removed except for that protecting the fuel tanks in the rear of the long engine nacelles, which housed either 266-horsepower Rolls-Royce Eagle II or 320-horsepower Sunbeam Cossack engines. The four-bladed propellers were of laminated walnut with the blade tips sheathed in brass.

The shorter nacelles of the O/400 were made possible by relocating the main fuel tanks to the interior of the fuselage, where two transversely mounted cylindrical tanks each held 130 Imperial gallons (156 U.S. gallons). Each tank had a single air-driven fuel pump to supply fuel to the engines. There were also two gravity fuel tanks in the leading edge of the upper wing center section, each holding twelve Imperial gallons (14.4 U.S. gallons). A fifteen-Imperial-gallon (18 U.S. gallons) oil tank was located in the rear of each engine nacelle.

Up to five defensive 0.303-caliber Lewis guns could be carried by the O/100 and O/400, with twin Lewis guns on a Scarff ring in the nose position. Early examples of both types had a single Lewis gun in a dorsal position, mounted on a bar extending the width of the fuselage, which allowed the gun to slide from side to side. When twin guns were introduced in this position, they were mounted on twin swivel mounts, one on each side. A seat was provided for the dorsal gunner.

There was also a trap door in the floor of the fuselage through which a gun could be fired. The floors of both these gun positions were made with wooden slats. Similar floors were provided for the front gunner's position and the cockpit. The pilot occupied the right cockpit seat and the observer the left. Both the O/100 and O/400 carried a radio set.

Up to a total of eight 112-pound bombs could be carried by the O/100. The O/400 could carry sixteen 112-pound bombs, three 550-pound bombs, or one 1,605-pound bomb in the bomb bay, located in the main center section of the fuselage. A rack for light bombs, which could be manually dropped, was located behind the cockpit seats.

The wings of both the O/100 and O/400 were constructed in panels, five for the top wing and four for the bottom, with box-type main and rear spars and steel tube engine mounts. Between the main and rear spars were three interspars. Each wing section had four evenly spaced steel tube compression members. Wing ribs were of built-up lattice construction, except those at the wing folds, which were solid. There were partial ribs between each main rib. All interplane struts were of plywood-covered spruce.

The main landing gear was sprung with rubber bungee cord under generous wooden fairings. Main landing gear tires were either 800 cm x 150 cm or 900 cm x 200 cm.

The Handley Page V/1500 was of similar construction, the chief difference, besides its larger size, being its four tandem-mounted Rolls-Royce Eagle VIII engines of 375 horsepower each in twin nacelles. The rear engine in each nacelle drove a four-blade pusher propeller, and the forward engine in each drove a two-blade tractor propeller.

The V/1500 was unusual for the period in having a defensive gun mounted in the extreme tail, giving the gunner an unprecedented field of fire with his single .303-caliber Lewis gun on a 'rocking post' mounting. The other defensive gun positions in the nose and dorsal positions had twin Lewis guns on Scarff No. 2 mounts. A V/1500 was also used in late 1918 to test the installation in the mid-upper gunner's position of a 3-inch mortar, which could fire shells over the bomber's tail into the path of a pursuing enemy fighter. This device was not adopted.

The maximum bomb load of the V/1500 was 7,500 pounds, but on a typical mission to Berlin the bomb load would have been approximately a thousand pounds.

The Vickers Vimy, like the O/100 and O/400, was designed as a strategic heavy bomber, despite its being smaller than its Handley page 'cousins.' Its construction of wire-braced timber was usual for the period, but it departed from convention in its use of steel tube for the forward fuselage and McGruer hollow spars for the aft fuselage.

The Vimy's wings, both top and bottom, were constructed in three panels, the middle panel spanning the distance between the engines. Only the outer panels had dihedral.

The design of the Vimy enabled it to carry its bomb loads vertically within the fuselage in twelve cells between the front and rear spars. Eight bombs could also be carried externally on rails under the wing center section, immediately inboard of the landing gear. A maximum bomb load of 4,804 pounds could be carried, although contemporary records state that a typical combat load was approximately 2,000 pounds. An alternate load was a pair of twelve-inch torpedoes under the forward fuselage.

Defensive armament of the Vimy consisted of four Lewis guns mounted in pairs on Scarff rings in the nose and dorsal positions, although the dorsal guns were not usually fitted postwar. Six spare ammunition drums were carried for the nose guns, four for the dorsal guns.

The version of the Vimy produced in the greatest numbers was powered by a pair of 360-horsepower Rolls-Royce Eagle VIII water-cooled engines driving wooden four-blade propellers.

G-EATH, formerly O/400 D4631, was converted to O/10 configuration in 1920 for use by Handley Page Transport, which operated it on the Zurich-to-London route until September 1923, when it was withdrawn and left to slowly rot away behind the hangars at Croydon.

Delivered civilianized as an O/10 in the summer of 1920, ex-RAF O/400 D4609 is seen here at Croydon in September 1921. It was withdrawn in January two years later. Lettering on the nose reads "Handley Page Transport, London."

▲ Another view of G-EATM at Croydon when in use by Handley Page. The conversion number 'HP-42' is on the extreme end of the fuselage.

▼ Carrying the conversion number 'HP-43,' Handley Page O/10 G-EATN was O/400 J2261 with the RAF until July 1920. It was withdrawn from service on European passenger routes and broken up in May 1922.

The first of the O/10 conversions, this aircraft, wearing an overall aluminum dope finish and carrying the conversion code 'H.P. 34,' had been O/400 F308. It was registered G-EASX in October 1920 before being sold abroad in April 1931.

▲ One of only four F.B.28 Vimy Commercials registered in Great Britain, G-EASI was flown by Instone Airlines. The Vimy Commercial used the wings, tail, and engines of the former warplane with a new passenger fuselage.

▲ Also taken at Croydon some time after May 1920, this view of G-EASI shows the nosewheel landing gear, bloated fuselage, and name 'CITY OF LONDON' on the nose.

The Vickers Vimy Commercial

In 1919, Handley Page began manufacturing a civilian version of the Vimy, powered by Rolls-Royce Eagle engines but with a rotund monocoque spruce plywood fuselage to accommodate ten passengers. The crew of two sat in an open cockpit. Known as the Vimy Commercial, it was produced mainly for foreign customers. The Chinese government ordered one hundred, but only forty were completed, probably due to the customer's failure to pay interest after April 1922.

There were but four Vimy Commercials on the British civil register. These were: G-EAAV, which had originally carried the very early identity 'K107;' G-EASI, the Instone Company's 'City of London;' G-EAUL, which was sold to France in August 1921; and G-EAUY, which probably became J6864, the prototype for the RAF's Vernon troop carriers.

▶ Mail and freight being loaded aboard G-EASI, which wears the flag of operators Instone Airlines on its nose. When this machine was finally broken up its fuselage became a summer house in the nearby back garden of the Royal Dutch Airlines Area Manager! This is probably a publicity photo.

Above the Trenches

More World War I aircraft from Squadron/Signal Publications

1173 German Bombers of WW I

1167 Nieuport Fighters in action

1166 Fokker D.VII in action

1164 de Havilland D.H.9 in action

1158 Fokker Eindecker in action

1137 Bristol Fighter in action

1123 BE2 in action

1110 Sopwith Fighters in action

1098 Fokker Dr.I in action

For more information on Squadron/Signal books, visit www.squadron.com